GO FACTS NATURAL DISASTERS
Fire and Drought

A & C BLACK • LONDON

Fire and Drought

contents

© Blake Publishing 2006
Additional material © A & C Black Publishers Ltd 2006

First published in Australia in 2006 by Blake Education Pty Ltd

This edition published in the United Kingdom in 2006 by
A & C Black Publishers Ltd, 38 Soho Square, London W1D 3HB
www.acblack.com

Hardback edition
ISBN-10: 0-7136-7959-X
ISBN-13: 978-0-7136-7959-5

Paperback edition
ISBN-10: 0-7136-7967-0
ISBN-13: 978-0-7136-7967-0

A CIP record for this book is available from the British Library.

Written by Ian Rohr
Publisher: Katy Pike
Editor: Paul O'Beirne
Design and layout by The Modern Art Production Group

Photo credits: p7 (tr), p9 (bl, br), p11 (br), p13 (bl), p14 (tl), p17 (tr, bl),
p19 (tl, tr), p21 (tl, bottom), p23 (tr, bl) (australian picture library); p17 (tl, br),
p23 (tl) (aap). Illustration on p6: Toby Quarmby

Printed in China by WKT Company Ltd.

Fires

Fires are one of nature's most destructive and frightening events. Unlike other natural disasters, fires can be caused by forces of nature or by the actions of people.

Fires that burn in the bush or forest are known as bushfires, or forest fires. Small fires have benefits for plants and soil, but severe fires damage the environment for years. If fires burn out of control, they can also destroy homes and farms.

Natural causes

Lightning strikes are a common cause of fire. During hot and dry summers, lightning strikes can **ignite** 100 regional fires in a 24-hour period. It is estimated that in Australia, lightning strikes account for 25% of all bushfires, while in the United States, 50% of forest fires in the Rocky Mountains are caused by lightning.

Unnatural causes

Humans are responsible for some fires in the bush or forests. Camp fires that aren't **extinguished** properly, **burn-offs** getting out of control, carelessly-tossed cigarette butts and sparks from equipment and machinery all start fires. The other major way humans start fires is by deliberately lighting them. This reckless and criminal behaviour is known as **arson**.

There are about 15 000 bushfires in Australia each year.

There are harsh penalties, including prison sentences, for people who are caught starting fires deliberately.

GO FACT!

DID YOU KNOW?

Australia's hot, dry climate makes it one of the most fire-prone places on the planet. Sunshine and high temperatures make trees and grass very dry and easy to burn. Most Australian native plants burn quickly and easily.

5

How Fires Operate

Fires are unpredictable and can change very rapidly. However, we do understand the basic forces that control the **ignition** and behaviour of bush and forest fires.

The climate

Once a fire starts, climatic conditions either help or hinder the spread of the fire. High temperatures, low **humidity** and strong winds all increase the chance of a bushfire taking hold. The sun also heats **fuel** to ignition temperature. The lack of water in the air, caused by low humidity, adds to the danger. The wind adds the last ingredient that fires need – oxygen. The more wind, the more oxygen the fire receives. Winds can also carry burning embers that start new fires, known as spot fires, downwind.

The topography

Topography means the form of landscape, and this influences fire's behaviour. On level ground, a fire will burn outwards in a circular shape, provided there is no wind and an even distribution of fuel. On sloping ground a fire will burn faster when travelling up a slope. This is because winds tend to blow uphill, pushing the fire along. These factors cause fires to race up gullies and canyons. Once fires reach a high-**intensity** level, a crown fire may start when the fire travels quickly from treetop to treetop.

OXYGEN HEAT FUEL

The high oil content in the leaves of Australian eucalyptus trees makes them highly combustible.

Few bushfires travel faster than 25 km/h (16 mph), but that is still faster than most people can run.

GO FACT!

DID YOU KNOW?

Three things are needed to start a fire. A fire needs *fuel* such as trees, *oxygen* from the air and *heat*. This is known as the fire triangle.

Fires – Damage and Benefits

Fires cause widespread damage to human, animal and plant communities. Surprisingly, they can also have some benefits.

Damage

An intensely hot **firestorm** kills off huge areas of vegetation and the wildlife that lives there. Some of these will not recover. High-intensity fires also lead to soil erosion where there are no roots to hold the soil in place.

Animals that cannot get away from the fire will die from the heat, or the smoke. Some animals will survive but for them there is now less food available and less shelter from predators and **feral** animals.

Fire also destroys farms and houses. Fire damage can be very costly. In addition, the heavy smoke clouds from major fires can cause breathing difficulties.

Benefits

In Australia, many plants are adapted to fire, having seeds that only **germinate** after a fire. Most areas will regenerate completely after a fire. The fire's heat forces fruits to open, releasing their seeds. The ash that is left provides nutrients for the soil. Fires also **eradicate** plant diseases.

When a fire goes through an area, it removes old and dead plants, so new growth can occur. Low-intensity fires reduce the amount of fuel in an area. This limits the likelihood of more damaging high-intensity fires.

Major bushfires may continue to burn for months, until they either run out of fuel, or are extinguished by changes in the weather or by the efforts of people.

Fire does not always 'destroy' the forest, but rather damages it.

GO FACT!

DID YOU KNOW?

The massive Indonesian bushfires of 1997–1998 created a smoke cloud that covered much of South East Asia. The thick cloud caused a passenger airliner to crash, killing all 234 people on board.

How We Fight Fires

Firefighters use a variety of equipment to control fires. Fire-fighting equipment ranges from backpack style water sprayers through to planes and helicopters.

Fighting fires

Many countries use fire prevention strategies such as **hazard reduction burns** and **firebreaks** to reduce the chance of fires. When fires threaten property, teams of professional and volunteer firefighters combine to try and control the fire. Individuals may also join the struggle to try and save their homes and farms.

Fire-fighting equipment and techniques

Sprays are used to put out smaller spot fires, while large tankers, holding up to 4000 litres of water, are used on bigger fires.

Planes and helicopters bomb fires with thousands of litres of water. Sometimes foam or chemicals are mixed with the water to help slow the fire. Aircraft are also used for mapping and transporting fire crews.

In the US firefighters parachute into an area near a fire. They are know as smokejumpers. Fire fighting equipment is also dropped. The 'jumpers' cut a firebreak. When the fire is contained, the jumpers help to **'mop-up'**. Afterwards the jumpers hike to the nearest road to be collected.

There are over 300 smokejumpers working in the United States.

A helicopter can carry from 400 to 9000 litres of water in buckets suspended underneath the chopper.

Volunteer firefighters receive training in all aspects of fire prevention, behaviour and fighting techniques, as well as detailed safety training.

GO FACT!

DID YOU KNOW?

Fire services and scientists in Australia are working on making fire tankers a safe place to shelter. If fire crews get overtaken by flames, sprinkler systems and heat-resistant windows have been developed to protect firefighters from the extremely dangerous **radiant heat**.

11

How We Fight Fires

Fighting fires demands planning and coordination. The emergency services need to work together when faced with a major fire.

Coordination

A great deal of planning and coordination is required when fighting fires. This serves the double purpose of keeping the firefighters and public safe, and making sure that all resources are being used in the most effective way. The tactics of fighting bush or forest fires are usually coordinated from a central command post, using wireless communications. This allows all firefighters to be aware of each other's movements and of what the fire is doing.

Help from afar

Battling major fires often requires more resources than one area is able to provide. When this occurs, firefighters from other counties or regions travel to the area to add their numbers and skills to the task. On some occasions firefighters have even travelled overseas, though this is more often to offer advice and **expertise** than to help fight the actual fire. At other times, firefighters have helped to bring one region's major fires under control, only to have to rush back to their own area to battle local outbreaks.

FIRE BRIGADE

Many organisations come together to fight fires and to help people affected by them. These include volunteer and regular fire brigades, the police and ambulance services, the armed forces and charity groups such as the Red Cross.

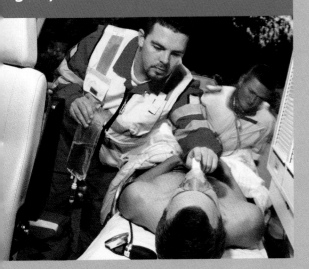

NO FIRES

EXTREME FIRE HAZARD

EFFECTIVE DATE: July 30/03

BY ORDER OF MINISTER

Part of fire management involves providing regular updates to the general public via the media.

Australia has over 250 000 volunteer firefighters, while the United States has about 750 000 volunteer firefighters.

13

How to Survive a Fire

In fire-prone countries such as Australia, knowing what to do in a bushfire will greatly increase your chances of survival. If you find yourself at risk of fire, the following procedures could help to save your life.

1. Protecting homes

Important tasks *before* the fire season include:

- Move **flammable** materials such as dead branches and petrol containers away from the house.
- Keep the lawns mowed and remove flammable shrubs and weeds.
- Remove leaves and sticks from gutters, eaves and decks.
- Check all taps and hoses are working.

2. Protecting people

- Wear clothing that covers all bare skin.
- Wear natural fibres, such as cotton denim, as they burn less easily.
- Wear shoes and a hat.
- Wear goggles and tie a bandanna or large handkerchief over mouth and nose to minimise effects of smoke.
- Drink plenty of water.
- Beware of falling branches.

3. When a fire approaches

- Block all downpipes and fill gutters with water.
- Hose down roof and side of house where fire is approaching.
- Pack essential items and important documents in case of evacuation.
- Fill baths, sinks and all available buckets with water, for drinking and putting out spot fires.
- Go inside and close all windows and doors when fire is close.
- Put wet towels and blankets against gaps around doors and windows.
- Stay inside until fire passes.
- Then go outside and check for spot fires.

4. What to do if you're trapped in a car

- Park in a clear area and stay in vehicle.
- Put headlights on so other vehicles can see you.
- Close all windows and vents.
- Switch off ignition.
- Lie on floor covered by woollen blanket or cotton towel.
- Drink water if available.
- Stay in vehicle until **fire front** passes.
- Ensure that fire front has passed before driving on.

In Australia, people live with the yearly threat of summer bushfires. Even major cities are threatened by raging fires.

Fire in the capital

On January 18th 2003, high temperatures and powerful winds combined to produce firestorms in the western suburbs of Canberra, the nation's capital city.

Authorities thought the fires would not threaten residents, but by mid-afternoon, the sky had turned red, and drivers had to use headlights because of the smoke.

Jumping across firebreaks, the fires roared into the bushy south-western suburbs. Local radio sounded an emergency signal and broadcast a list of threatened suburbs. The government declared a state of emergency. Some suburbs were evacuated as firefighters and homeowners fought desperately to save houses. Fire-fighting helicopters water bombed the fires to try to slow their progress.

Gale force winds fanned the fires. These winds kept changing direction, which caused the fire front to keep growing. Flames stripped the roofs and windows from houses. By the time the flames had died and the smoke began to clear over 350 homes had been reduced to ashes, another 200 damaged, and four people had lost their lives.

The tornadoes created by the flames swirled at speeds of over 200 km/h (124 mph).

The damage caused by the fires was estimated to be above AUD$250 million (£100 million).

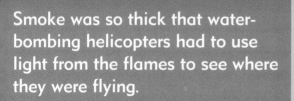

Smoke was so thick that water-bombing helicopters had to use light from the flames to see where they were flying.

GO FACT!

DID YOU KNOW?

One of the casualties of the fire was the historic Mt. Stromlo Observatory. The fire destroyed all five of the observatory's telescopes.

What Causes Droughts?

A drought is an extended period of less than average, or no rainfall. Droughts are caused by different climatic features.

Climatic causes

When hot, dry spells extend for long periods, severe drought can occur. These dry periods combined with high temperatures are usually caused by **high pressure air systems**. Rain is formed by **water vapour** rising when hot and cold air masses meet. The cooler air forces the warm air upward, where it cools, forming rain droplets. By preventing warm and cold air masses from meeting, high pressure air systems can maintain lengthy dry phases.

The El Niño factor

El Niño is a climatic feature that leads to droughts and flooding in the Southern Hemisphere. Normally, winds travel westwards across the Pacific Ocean from South America towards Australia, driving the warm ocean current in front of them. However, every five to seven years the winds and ocean current reverse. The warm water that usually travels west now heads towards South America, increasing the air's humidity and creating heavy rains and storms. In Australia, the lack of the warm, rain-producing current leads to reduced rainfall and an increased chance of drought.

On average, Australia suffers from a major drought every 10–20 years.

GO FACT!

DID YOU KNOW?

When the El Niño weather pattern reverses, Australia goes into drought, while on the other side of the Pacific flooding and storms occur.

'Drought' means different things in different countries. In the UK, 15 rainless days is classed as a drought, while in Canada it's 30 days. Droughts in these wetter, damp regions tend to last for weeks, or in extreme cases months, whereas droughts in places like Australia and Africa can last for years.

Major Droughts of the 20th Century

During the early 1900s, major droughts impacted on the people of Russia and the USA.

Famine in Russia (1932-1933)

In the early 1930s, the Russian regions of the Ukraine and the Volga were struck by drought. This in turn led to famine which claimed the lives of around five million people. Most were **peasants** who relied on farming for food. The Russian government of the time did not want to admit that they couldn't feed their own people, so they denied the famine existed and refused all offers of overseas aid.

The American Dust Bowl (1932-1940)

The American Midwest is an area prone to climate variations. It had been farmed and abandoned before, but good rainfall in the early 20th century encouraged a new generation to try their luck. When no rain fell in 1932, the crops failed and the topsoil dried to dust. This was then blown away by hot strong winds. Dust storms lasting for weeks buried roads and farms and turned day to night. By the time it rained again, in 1941, more than half the area's population had left in search of greener pastures.

Countless farmsteads in the Midwest had to be abandoned during the drought, as they were literally swallowed by dust and sand.

DID YOU KNOW?
Ukraine, known as the breadbasket of Europe, is a land famous for its fertile, black earth and its golden wheat. Yet, only last century, several million Ukrainians starved to death due to drought and famine.

Thousands of people died in the American Dust Bowl from starvation or lung diseases caused by the ever-present dust.

Despite advances in technology and science in the second half of the 20th century, droughts continued to impact on people. Two of the worst of these were in Africa and Australia.

Starvation in Ethiopia (1981–1985)

The Ethiopian drought was one of the 20th century's worst natural disasters. The drought caused crop failures which in turn led to famine. This, combined with a civil war raging in the country, led millions of people to abandon their homes in search of food and safety. As these **refugees** crowded into camps, conditions deteriorated. It was many months before the rest of the world knew how bad the situation was. By the time international aid began arriving, it was too late to save countless thousands of people.

A sunburnt country (1982–1983)

The Australian drought of 1982–1983 was short but sharp. Combining many of the 'classic' elements of a drought – heat, crop and stock losses, land erosion and dust storms – it also led to the severe Ash Wednesday bushfires that claimed 76 lives and left thousands homeless. The grim statistics of the drought include over AUD$3000 million (£1210 million) in damage and the death of millions of sheep and cattle.

A huge dust cloud dumped 10 000 tonnes of topsoil on the city of Melbourne in February 1983.

DID YOU KNOW?

The massive Live Aid rock concerts in Philadelphia and London were staged to help Ethiopia's drought victims. The concert was broadcast live on TV and radio to more than 1.5 billion people in 160 countries and raised over £80 million for famine relief.

Though it is impossible to calculate how many people died in the Ethiopian famine, it is estimated that at its height, 20 000 children died each month.

Droughts rarely lead to human deaths in developed nations. In countries where people rely on regular harvests for their survival, droughts lead to famine.

The Costs of Drought

Drought can cause enormous problems for farmers. In Australia, many people believe that farmers in harsh, dry regions should quit the land, as it is unsuited to farming.

Abandon the land

Many people have suggested farmers abandon their land, considering them crazy for staying when droughts are **inevitable**. When in drought, farmers get into debt as they have no crops and their hungry, thirsty livestock need food and water. If the drought is severe, the farmers may lose their livestock and their income. This means borrowing money.

Changing for the better

There are others who believe things could be better if farmers planted more trees and hedges. This would increase the moisture in the soil, as vegetation holds moisture. They also believe the flow of water on the land is important. By creating creeks and channels for irrigation, the fields could be watered naturally.

Staying put

Most farmers want to stay on their land, but they understand things need to change. This can be difficult as it takes money to change farming **techniques**. Unfortunately many farmers are forced off their land and lose everything as a direct result of drought.

Extended droughts can lead to deserts expanding into areas that were once fertile.

Farmers are being encouraged to leave stones in their fields because they create shade for seedlings.

FARM FOR SALE

In severe droughts, many farmers are forced to sell their homes and possessions, because the starving livestock and lack of crops leave them with no income.

GO FACT!

DID YOU KNOW?

Exceptionally heavy rains often come immediately after a drought, leading to the reverse problem – major flooding.

25

Droughts and Wildlife

A sustained drought can have a devastating impact on wildlife populations.

A struggle to survive

Many animals that live in drought-prone regions have adapted to the dry conditions. However, an extended, severe drought will eventually affect them. As grasses and other plants die from lack of water, grazing animals face greater competition for food. Farm animals compete with wildlife for food and water. Often farmers will kill large numbers of wild animals in order to allow their stock greater access to whatever food remains.

Most living creatures can survive for much longer without food than they can without water. As waterholes and creeks dry up, more and more animals gather around the remaining water supplies. This not only increases the competition for food, but also makes them more vulnerable to predators. Predators find it increasingly difficult to survive, as animals which they normally prey on, die of starvation.

DID YOU KNOW?

One of Australia's best-known animals, the kangaroo, adapts in an interesting way to help it cope with droughts. During particularly dry seasons, female kangaroos stop reproducing. By keeping the population down individuals face less competition for food and a greater chance of survival.

During long droughts, large flocks of inland-dwelling birds often move to the coast and cities in search of food and water.

Many African animals eat the moist bark of the baobab tree during times of drought.

27

Drought Survival Techniques

People can help conserve water and lessen the drought's impact. Droughts end when enough rain falls on an affected area.

In the country

As reservoirs dry up and water levels fall, farmers must try to find ways to keep their stock and crops alive. Reservoirs and irrigation help for a time, but in a really severe drought the reservoirs dry up and there is no water left for irrigation. When this happens, farmers often graze their sheep and cattle by the roadside. However, unless the rains come, farmers can do little but buy feed and watch their crops die.

In the city

Though city dwellers are less affected by droughts than those who live in the country, an extended dry period can still impact on their lives. In order to help ease the strain on dwindling reservoirs, councils and governments often

introduce water restrictions. These can range from light restrictions to total bans on activities such as washing the car with a hose, or using garden sprinklers. Some city councils are also making it compulsory for new homes to have water tanks.

Even in drought-free times, people should make an effort to use less water.

Farmers can help their land handle dry periods more effectively by not cutting down too many trees. Trees help the soil retain its moisture.

Councils encourage people to use less water for household needs. Some activities are banned, such as watering the garden, until the drought eases.

GO FACT!

DID YOU KNOW?

Water is one of our planet's most vital resources, but people the world over, particularly those in developed nations, use far more than they really need.

29

Famous Droughts of the Past

When	Where	Effects
1895–1903	Australia	The 'King Drought' at the turn of the century is regarded as the worst in the country's history. It killed five million cattle, 52 million sheep, sent thousands of farmers bankrupt and at its height affected most of the nation.
1900	India	It is estimated that over three million people died due to drought, starvation and disease.
1921–1922	Russia	Affected the Ukraine and the entire Volga region. Caused widespread famine which led to the deaths of millions of people.
1928–1930	China	Famine results in over three million deaths.
1936	China	Five million people starved to death and 34 million farmers were forced off their land.
1941	China	Over 2.5 million people died due to starvation and disease.
1962	Brazil	A seven-month drought was followed by huge fires that killed 250 people, left 300 000 people homeless, and destroyed most of Brazil's important coffee crop.
1967–1970	Nigeria	A famine that was caused by drought and made worse by an armed conflict with neighbouring Biafra affected over eight million people.
1968–1972	Iran	Iran suffered a severe drought that ended in a blizzard. As people were unprepared, 4000 died from the cold and snow.
1969–1974	Mali	A severe drought killed over a million people through the combined effects of starvation and disease. An estimated four million cattle also perished.
1972	India	Over 800 people died when 14 Indian states suffered a month-long heatwave with temperatures exceeding 43°C. Most died of starvation when their crops withered.
1992	Zimbabwe	The El Niño phenomenon led to a drought that caused food shortages over southern Africa and affected 30 million people.
1994	Australia	A drought reduced New South Wales' wheat crop by 90% and covered 93% of the state. It also affected much of southern Queensland.
1997	New Guinea	A drought combined with a freeze destroyed the essential sweet potato crops and dried up the Fly River. Sixty people died and over 700 000 were affected.

Glossary

arson the deliberate burning of property

burn-offs burning vegetation to clear the land

eradicate to get rid of or destroy

expertise a great deal of knowledge about a subject

extinguished put out

feral wild or untamed

firebreaks areas of land which are cleared and ploughed to stop fire from spreading by removing its fuel

fire front the edge of the fire which leads the flames

firestorm raging fire of great intensity, often with tornado-like winds

flammable easy to catch fire

fuel material that allows fire to burn, such as grass, leaves and sticks

germinate to begin growing or developing

hazard reduction burns controlled fires lit to reduce or remove fuel in a particular area

high pressure air systems the weight of the air around us is known as its pressure. Cold air sinks, compressing the air below it and causing higher pressure. High pressure systems prevent rain from forming by stopping water vapour rising and forming clouds.

humidity the amount of water vapour in the air. Low humidity means a low level of water vapour.

ignite to set on fire

ignition bursting into flames

inevitable unable to be avoided

intensity amount of energy released by the fuel as it burns

mop-up fire is completely extinguished by smothering any flames with soil

peasants people who farm their own tiny farms, or work as farm-labourers for land-owners. Throughout history they have been poor and powerless.

radiant heat the heat that comes from a fire

refugees people forced to leave their area or country because of war or political unrest

techniques ways of doing something

water vapour water in the form of a gas as opposed to a liquid

Index